Walkways

Derek Seymour

Walkways © Derek Seymour 2022.

The moral rights of the Author have been asserted.

ISBN: 978 1 9163392 1 7

Published by Blackrock Publishing, Number 1 Tanglewood, Pottery Road, Dun Laoghaire, Co. Dublin A96X2C5.
Advice on Typesetting and Layout – Joe Bergin
Cover Design, Graphics and Typesetting - Joshua Seymour.
Photography © Derek Seymour 2022.

Acknowledgements

A number of these poems have appeared in publications viz; 'Celebrating the Gift of Life' 2018 Ed. Nick Park; 'Cornucopia - Carraig Dubh Writers' Group Anthology 2019' Ed. Leo Cullen; 'Cathalbui Poetry Competition 2021 Anthology of Selected Entries'; Skylight 47 Magazine; Books Ireland; The Methodist Newsletter; ArtServe Magazine; The Candlestick Magazine; St. Patrick's People Magazine.

"O for a beaker full of the warm South"

John Keats
Ode to a Nightingale

CONTENTS

Sense of Place

My Fair City

What do you remember great-grandad?
It's long ago but Reckitt's blue and Raddle red
preserved my smudged thumb prints, my human
stain
on dank walls of shared halls, the stairwells of that
time.

I lived the photos of '09, child poverty clear on cinder
smeared faces,
barefooted children stared-down-on by black-
shawled mothers
and flat-capped fathers who worked as Tuggers,
Carters, Dockers,
herded cattle on the North Wall for Birkenhead and
Manchester
where they learned and shared that happy kids sing
'The Alley Alley O',
when big ships sail at high tide on the last day of
September.

Some survived the lock-out fuel famine of '13
burning the banisters to kindle a fire,
and under their dad's buttoned blankets
thin arms sought other arms to anchor warmth.

In the '60's, I recoiled from York Street's dark doors,
foul smelling hallways, housing 'unfit for human
habitation',
while the Salvation Army hostel served hot meals to
residents,

passers-by, tenement boys, with the Friday special,
fried-eggs,
green peas and chips followed by the comfort of
sponge pudding
coated with yellow hot sweet steamy custard and,
promises of rehousing.

In the garden of the King's Inns gnarled life absorbed
a wrought-iron frame;
denied rest to seat seekers and as a curiosity Japanese
tourists
snapped the grotesque to show folks back home that
strange things happen
where inner-city residents hardly notice a tree that
eats a chair.

Christmas Eve, St. Patrick's Cathedral, Dublin

Decani and Cantoris unite to sing, 'Drop down, ye
heavens, from above and',
sing, 'let the skies pour down righteousness,' sing,
'let the earth open and'
sing, 'let them bring forth salvation.'
while in my top-coat, wedged warmly in a good pew
I think indeed *expectans expectavi dominum.*

Above and around me darkest green and reddest
holly wreaths sprinkled
with white berried mistletoe wait as on tiptoe for
creation's fulfilment.
The smell of woodland pine freshens the air, a soft
ripple of wind stirs
strands of my hair as Pentecostal tongues of fire
might hover and gently alight
on those faithful, saddened 'because there was no
room in the inn'.

Later, Dupre's B major from Opus seven thunders
from the organ loft and as if giving birth
the great West door flung-open, delivers
the clamorous warmth into December's cold night air
while the cacophony of wildest bells jolt my senses.

Sentinel robed clergy stand
ready to catch an eye, touch an arm,
brush a coat-tail of even slightest acquaintance,
validating existence, giving reassurance of new birth
for indeed I think *Hodie Christus Natus Est.*

Old James' Street Workhouse (1707-1826)

A metal cradle
suspended in the
stout wood gate
to rotate between
within and without
where unwanted foundlings
are placed in care
to ensure few survive.

Café Society

There's a riotous buzz in the Cafe
this morning, all human life is here,
bright-eyed babies in buggy-cars,
one teething on a silver spoon,
full bosomed mummies muffling
crying kids, wiping runny noses
while granny sits propped by pillows
and cushions.

In a corner two guys
engage over steam-hot mint teas
while another two lovers pledge constancy,
she with sunglasses stylishly perched
on well-groomed hair,
he, dressed to impress,
their eyes,
locked, unblinking.

In the ante room the rowing team
have commandeered all the tables
their loud chatter, of victories and missed
opportunities.

Famed pictures of broken chairs
decorate the white stucco walls
and outside under Perspex canopy
there is a reassured murmur
of conversation, a hum of well-being
as day-trippers loll in wicker chairs,
catching the eyes

of waitresses dressed in smart
pale blue tea shirts and snug tight
denim blue-jeans.

The Manageress,
mobile phone tucked firm
in her jeans back pocket,
rules imperiously, proudly
she exudes, 'this is my Café'.

Brahms and Clara

Enfold me in your lush harmonies,
the texture of the cello range
where the heart beats and rests,
impassioned voice,
unrequited breath,
the timbre of the full orchestra
playing fortissimo.

Glenstal Abbey

Through electric gates the seeker enters the rolling
estate.
The narrow drive winds through well-tended fields
toward the oak-treed horizon.

Ramp signs say
'slow' and 'slower'.
Gardeners, carpenters, tradesmen are directed to
other routes.

Behind a copse, battlements confront the seeker.
From the high tower a watchman
has turned to stone in the falling dusk.

Through portcullis gates, manicured lawns
display wooden seats engraved
with old names.

The empty refectory remembers
past sustenance, silent contemplation,
echoes of readings and music imbibed.

The oratory
awaits the office of compline,
the night prayer of the church.

Soft diapason and dulciana fade as
a gentle bell chimes and
the sweet smell of incense lingers.

Monks in robes, brown and cream,
ghost across the sanctuary,
seeking stalls to lay weary heads.

Silence holds,
while still the signs say
'slow' and 'slower'.

End of Day

In a soft chamois pouch
smooth as stones from Kidron's Brook
jade green, midnight blue, dark cherry-red,
cloudy sworled cat's eyes,
the indestructible steelie,
tossed and rolled by un-gloved
kid's bruised knuckles,
enraptured by thwack and crack of the strike
while grandads toss
unexploded cannon balls
shout 'Pétanque', at the clack of steel on steel
as they slay imagined Goliaths
on village greens
with their end of days.

Disturbance

The Lift

Exhaling, it judders to a halt.
I slide back the metal gate,
the concertina of collapsing diamonds
fails to snare me.

Foot forward on an unsteady floor
I close the lattice behind me
and hear the satisfying clack.
The single Solus bulb flickers,
its power source fluctuates.
The air in the lift is stifling
my chest is tight with anxiety.

I press the green starter button,
hear the hydraulic drive build courage,
the whirr of sound is a comfort,
the gentle rock a reassurance
all will be well.

I know the plunge,
will throw my stomach into my mouth
and always my hand hovers close
on the red button.

The walls of the shaft are smooth.
I pray the safety ledges, engraved at intervals
provide enough grip to secure the failsafe lock,
though I fear the old machinery is unreliable,
incapable of forestalling the plunge.

Beyond the basement I know there is the pit
and in the slime the creature lurks
waiting in darkness with gravity,
its irresistible friend.

When the plunge happens,
I will pound the red button,
hear the squeal as cables snap taut,
feel the lurch as tension spits and squeezes
moisture from life sinews.

Before the pit, I know there is a side-line tunnel
which can divert away.
I pray for this diversion,
though it will take me away
too far ever to walk back.

Baby Doherty

On a grey slab plinth
at the station end of Talbot Street
I read
victims of Dublin and Monaghan bombings 1974.

With modern inoculation
I'm deadened to the names, their fates.

Then at foot,
nearest ground
I read
'Baby Doherty',

denied life,
denied birth.

Who Minds the House

When I am old, like mam and dad
I will know the things they know
and do better things
like work in an office or shop
or McDonald's, or Burger King
and get paid money.

For the moment, I don't do much - I help with 'jobs'
like, tidy my room space,
mind my toys,
try to keep my own stuff safe.
I don't eat 'greens' like broccoli or cabbage
but, when I'm older this will change.

I like to hang- out with cool guys
like Ryan and Cameron,
talk about girls and what they do,
watch Simpsons, Friends and Big Bang Theory,
have week-end sleep-overs, eat popcorn and crisps,
stay-up later than 'lights-out' at eight o'clock.

Most of the time she shouts, a lot,
calls him names, calls him a word - I think it's
halcololic.

Tonight I am minding the house on my own.
Like older people do.

Just the way it was

Cold November and my breath
fogs the window. I stand closer, exhale
until the blur blocks my vision.

I remember knitting needle
aerial antennae, angled,
to receive black and white TV signals.

Our 'News', read by Charles Mitchell with
pictures of a tired but confident man as
he reviewed troops with practiced salute.

Later, on CBS News,
America's most trusted man, Walter Cronkite
as he struggled to hold back tears.

The lady in pink jacket,
matched hat and red roses,
the Lincoln Continental's presidential pendants,
limp.

Over turf-fires in Ireland mantelpiece pictures
vied for pride of place as cold ashes clung
to hands unable to rekindle dead fires.

Eyesight dimmed but memory clear
I breathe again on the window pane.
In a calculated act I draw the letter K.

The Virus

I read McCarthy's *Road,*
King's *Stand,*
and Steinbeck's *Grapes.*

I feared a tipping point,
having to leave at short notice,
pack a car with essentials
for a post-apocalyptic world.

Not knowing the day nor the hour,
like the five wise virgins,
I prepared, ready to leave
at the drop of a hat.

Stocking a container with long life staples,
tuna, salt, bottled water and honey as I knew
ancient Egyptians had embalmed in this
and millennia later the sweetness remained.

A small battery operated radio, flint, torch,
mirror for signaling and my Swiss Army knife.
A Gideon *New Testament with Psalms*
and lastly, the essential Bear Grylls' *Ultimate Survival
Handbook.*

But the Government's instruction
said 'Stay at Home'.
All my escape preparations confounded
by the smallest of miscalculations.

Pathétique

From a side-balcony overlooking the swirl of sound,
you in grey herringbone tweed blazer,
long dark tartan skirt, equestrian patterned silk scarf,
with questions about the poverty of the composer
who would never hear this last work performed
and how his marriage could never work
and what was the essence of Russian nationalism
and the Radio Berlin Symphony Orchestra GDR
(thirty one months before the wall came down)
and such sense of being part of history with
Tchaikovsky's foreboding Symphony Pathetique
with its four movements inevitably ending *'ritenuto*
and *pppp'*.

The Lioness in Winter

Pacing on padded feet she smiles
Eyes dimmed by the cage of past years
The sounds she hears are distant
She must lip-read to understand the occasional word.

There was a time, on a bicycle
With child seat strapped to its back
Helter-skelter, here, there,
Delivering, visiting, collecting, meeting
When nothing daunted her mastery of her universe,
Indefatigable, invincible.

In the secure ward of the best nursing home
Though all mean well, all act well,
Her world shrinks smaller and smaller.

She who begat lions and lionesses
Buried a husband
Tamed demons, inspired saints
Feared none but the eternal
Now wonders if today is Thursday
And asks this so many times

With slippered feet and dressing gown
Rugged features, vacant eyes
The lioness in winter, waits and tonight,
There is a new star in Andromeda.

Animal Crackers

Friend or Foe

In a porcelain cup
within the white concave
I find the smallest spider
curled
and no place to hide.

Normally I squash and wash
without a thought
but
I remember being told that
spiders eat bugs, clean up after us.

In these distracted times
ever so gently
I tip my little friend
onto a potted plant leaf
and wish him well on his way.

Husky

Strolling the West pier,
glancing up I saw
the iconic creature
pulling ahead of its walker,
straining the harness,
full-bodied, confident, leading,
determined as only a husky can be,
going straight for the horizon,
not to stop 'till she drop
and in the heat of a summer's day,
her winter coat left behind,
she was still a wolf
taking her owner
for a walk.

Black Bobby (Mixed Breed Jack Russell Terrier)

Bounces, bounds on the stony beach
over rocks and sea-weeded pools
a sock in his mouth
he tosses and catches
the floppy foot piece
tail wagging, unflagging he circles
the centre of attention
where barefoot dad, two boys
and mom chase him round,
round and round, they shout
'bring back the sock Bobby, bring it back'

Uncaring, his joy unbounded,
unbundled in the moment,
a dog's paradise on this stony beach.

Mackerel

Three confined in a boat,
they sway extended rods
then, a shout of 'strike' as reel squeals
with sea-water zinging off taught line
and the strain of three fish hooked on feathers,
silver catching sunlight and the boat
bobbing on a restless swell off Shenick Island
where that Gifford girl died, swimming,
but at low-tide visitors can walk there,
and back again.

Later cleaned and gutted dipped in flour
fried fresh on a sizzling pan
with squeezed lemon,
we share rare precious harmony.

Gold Pelican

Words on a page,
my blue ink stains
cream writing paper.
Darker words drain me
while like a blood donor
I give
and give again
until it fits
the page
and there it is,
the poem.

Sheep

Seven sheep in the fenced-off field
dozy enough, waiting, clubbed together.
One gambols
with hop skip kick of hind legs
defying gravity and
together they scarper away.

At evening they crowd the fence again,
waiting, while two
head-butt each other insincerely.

It's just what sheep do.

Wasp

Zinging, the wasp hangs in warm air
between earth and sky
intensely waiting for earth to turn
for this wasp will not turn itself.

If time slowed I would see
wasp wings vibrate in the still air
know
like a Sikorsky helicopter
or Amazon drone,
the stillness of the centre
suspended by such sensitive liftings
of gossamer filament.

On Your Toes

Deus Ex Machina

Geometric patterns across a manicured expanse.
The soft motor murmuring as it nudges the
perimeter.
Then *volte face*, a new course set,
it consumes grass
as an automated sheep
without dung,
hums quietly all day,
criss-crosses the lawn
while I ignore the sign 'your feet are killing me',
and for a moment, I think I can explain
the mystery of crop circles,
and a universe with a place
for the *Husqvarna Automower*.

Dancer

Burnished long strong fingers
silver ringed thumb
nails coloured autumn.

Dark page-boy hair
framed brown eyes
sun-nourished complexion.

Denim jacketed
Long skirted
Free spirited.

New Age
Thin
Trendy.

Intoxicating
Engaging
Earthy.

Open sandaled.

Broken toes.

Tango - Por Una Cabeza ('by the head of a horse')

He holds her so lightly
Secure in his darkness
They move on the dance floor
To lose by a head

His senses enfold her
Four powerful reactors
Float light on the dance-floor
Glide smooth through the night

Poised still at his centre
In iconic tango
She melts to his rhythm
Her scent smouldering.

Jolly Hockey Sticks

From a yellow line at Sandymount Dart,
I see the game as Pembroke girls
battle green on black,
swarming the Astroturf,
configuring side against side,
marking, attacking, forward strutting
short skirts, knee socks, shin guards
and at the other end
a resting goalie
clad head to toe waits,
hearing the click-clack
of sticks and whistle tweets,
then, thud on wood,
this time, the visitor wins.

Percy

My father sang tenor in church and cathedral choirs,
at dinners, and occasionally major roles
in the minor oratorios of Maunder and Stainer.

His Gilbert and Sullivan duets were
'Take a pair of sparkling eyes' and 'We run them in'
and Handel solo versions of 'Where'er You Walk'
and not seeing his lady, 'Silent Worship'.

As children we watched Brendan O'Dowda
in monochrome on RTE singing his tributes
to the great Percy. 'Shlathery's Mounted Fut',
'The Mountains of Mourne', 'Eileen Oge',
and 'Are ye right there Michael?'

My father recorded these songs on spool reels
on a hot and humming Philips deck
which clicked, clacked and buzzed like in that movie
'The Ipcress File'.

During a rendering of 'Long long ago in the fields of
Gortnamona'
he told me Percy had lost his wife
and being so very young,
I thought this carelessness.

Old Boots

Van Gogh painted them
rugged on ochre background,
well- travelled, the laces crumpled,
worn from fastidious fingers,
discarded now near the door-mat,
with hardened leather
discouraging soft feet.

So many miles of stories,
walk one more mile with me?

Soles worn thin,
no use in wet weather,
memories of journeys,
paths trodden
conversations overheard.

Old boots,
discarded, as I walk away.

Mix and Match

Odd socks crumpled
in the corner, one
black one grey
orphaned from
life-long partners
thrown together
in careless abandon
when washed
the tumble took one,
then another, chewing the twins,
what hope now unless a colour-blind
seeker will match them through chance,
ignorance, on such their future hangs.

Seascapes

Ukulele Bus Busk
Saturday 25th August 2018 - for Joan

A long way from Honolulu
to the Eblana Club Dun Laoghaire
where the open-topped bus
collected sixty-nine enthusiasts
strumming in unison as would-be members
of the George Formby Society,
followers of Tiny Tim,
tiptoeing through the tulips
of the People's Park
paying fifteen euro
for their seats
to tour the coastal hostelries
with pineapples, garlands and friends
this frabjous day enthralled,
infatuated, as Lear's Owl who
looking up, sang to a small guitar.

But, Conrad's *horror*, road closed,
traffic diverted, entry denied,
Dublin city, all in lock-down.

And coming from the north-side
I cannot pass-over,
the Pope got in the way.

Dun Laoghaire Pier

Crab arms of the harbour
Shelter against an immensity of sea
Red and green pulse from pier ends
Warning of rocks while signaling safety.

Between Bandstand and Boyd
An un-minded Newfoundland dog
Meanders inconsolable,
Searching for his lost master.

Lovers holding hands
Occidental tourists
Lone walkers
Sitters, staring, smoking.

The girl playing mandolin
Melancholy music for
Dirty old town and *The girl I left behind me.*
Her woolly hat collecting tossed coins.

Across the harbour, constant clack
Ropes and stays against metal masts
Chatter incessantly.
Tethered yachts, strain for freedom.

Next Wednesday morning
Early, as her day begins she's leaving home
With her woolly hat carefully packed
In her travel-bag of memories.

Back of the House

Fifty years on
I flinch unearthing a deep buried metal casket
imprinted 'private' and within it, a photograph;
two happy people posed on a beach
near a lighthouse with soft sloped sand dunes,
all haloed by the blue sky of summer memories;
the moment captured as the breeze swept
hair strands against a shy smile.

I remember the sound of ocean lap lapping
on soft brown sand and on my lip, the taste of salt;

I had chosen to forget all this
but strange what lies buried behind this house.

I remember now,
I was the photographer.

Mortality Tables

I drew a line from Antarctica's
Mount Erebus to Alaska's Arctic.
The Google told me it was ten thousand miles
as a crow might fly, if a crow could fly that far.

The Southern ocean, steel-grey,
heaves, immense and daunting
as it births a mountainous wave.

Gestated, it passes Polynesia, Micronesia,
Tahiti, Samoa, Easter Island, through warm
Capricorn
to Cancer towards Hawaii, then Midway.

It travels north, seeking home-shore,
energy transferred, expended on
unflinching-rock and forlorn sands
dissipating, weakening, fading
to ripple gently in my old age
on Alaska's Aleutian Islands
in a cold-Bering Sea.

Coliemore Idyll

Between island and pier a heaving sea
breathes slow through Dalkey Sound.

The island, green and slate grey,
trails a residue of rocks.
Its watchtower signals shore
where triangulating cannons
sink imagined invaders.

Blue and half-blue meet a brighter horizon.
A singular gull catches a thermal, lifting it
toward the sanctuary where the
sea swallows rest before their African odyssey.

I smell seaweed and bladder wrack,
remember the taste of samphire
served with fresh fish in fashionable
Sandycove restaurants.

Passing cloud-shadows creep along the pier,
the blue-grey is darker now, still immense, fixating.

I break my gaze, my seascape reverie over.

Visions

'On a fine day you can see Wales'
says the plaque on the freshly painted
wood bench, watching over Killiney Bay.
From tired bespectacled eyes
on this clearest of clear days
when dark blue sea gently meets light blue sky
I strain, but see no promised land
but from a high point along this coast
on the brow of a hill,
atop a father's sturdy shoulders
a young child is told
'you can see Wales from here'
and only with a child's keen vision
the reply, yes, yes Dad, I can, I can see it, from here.

Killiney Beach

Sunlight skimming flat off crystal Sea
and smiles and charms of friends to be

Speckled stones
Wooden boats
Fishing tack
Buoys and ropes

Bronzed stout men with their flat caps
Who smoked Woodbines and swore mildly

Who dawn awakes
Who must obey the sea's call
To visit and reclaim lobsters from pots
Beyond the horizon

And return safe
Stronger for their journey, salt-hardened, satisfied.

Pilgrimage

Anna Akhmatova (1889-1966)
In Memoriam

Execute my husband, send our son to a Gulag, send
my partner too,
such purges should make an Odessa women recant
her words,
deny me a living when you expel me from the Union
of Soviet Writers
still, I will recite my *Requiem* as I stand for 300 hours
outside a Leningrad prison where they never open
the doors to me
and Russia oppressed under the tyres and screams
of Black Marias and still five thousand people will
attend my funeral.

It's Autumn Already

Blackberries
on long acre
ripe for plucking
full bloodied to burst
hung from thorn stems
snaring innocent hands
as they fill metal biscuit boxes
with fruit of childhood memories.

Friendship

Will the wind forget your dear face
Or still waters store your memory
Does the road recall soft footprints
Or chill raindrops fashion tears?
Journey on as Thomas tells us
Rage, yes rage against the night
Not weakened by the snares of others
Or the burdens we have shared
You my strength, my consolation
You my strongest confidante,
At my side in times of trouble
Dearest friend, my inspiration
Together forward into light, ever be
My best companion as the evening turns to night.

The Big Event

Quiet, away from madding crowds
the village sleeps undisturbed, its
tea-rooms, closed for renovation.

All road signs point starkly to other places, away.

The river, dark, brown, flanked with decaying foliage
flows under stone bridge, it meanders, deep,
with slow-swirl of eddies, banked by earthy smells.

The country church, filled with guests, pulses with
talk.

Rarely, such numbers fill this space
Betjeman's good church mouse
hides uncertain, hesitant of his place today.
Brief invaders one and all,
they will not return they will not stay.

Centre-aisle, the red carpet leads to the gilded
sanctuary.
Lilies, roses, drape the chairs where front and centre
they will sit,
sweetest scents from flowers mix with
the cold damp dust smell living here.

Parents, proudly dressed, wait in reserved pews,
Guests and visitors sport garnished lapels.

A string quartet from the gallery sets the tone,

the organist adjusts his music engrossed
in a booklet checking verses to be played.

The Minister of Religion, now robed and warmer
waits while
in his mind he rehearses the solemn words which
bind till parting.

The groom, nervous, sits with occasional words to
his best of men.
Two bridesmaids attired in emerald green chatter
nervously in the side aisle.

There is a shuffle, a slight breeze stirs.

All stand,
Hallelujah!
The Bride arrives.

Ardens sed Virens

In the high Sierra Nevada
stand earth's oldest living things
unsullied in the stillness,
clean, pure,
in the scent of woodland and wilderness.

Planted giant feet,
as footsteps suspended in time.

Widest girths soar to dizzying heights,
spectacular even in this California.

Around them, firm, the comfort
of layered soft wood mulch.
Vegetation scorched grey,
twigs, pine needles, brittle branches,
strewn in homage.

Redwoods tried by fire, not consumed,
burned yet flourishing, rejuvenated by flames.

The inner voice whispers
'Shoes off, Holy ground.'
Stand in awe,
Listen.

Pit Stop

The black python weighs heavy in my hands,
sturdy, muscular, its silver head glistens in sunlight
as the air shape-shifts around me.

Charmed, I swipe my card and inhale
the sweet poisonous scent and
swoon as lead-tinged fumes catch my throat.

I squeeze the handle and shoot.
I hear the slosh and gurgle
then the click of a full belly.

I wrest the heavy snake from the hole,
replace the head carefully
in the metal holster. Still charmed, I drive away.

Retail Therapy

Arabica Honduran coffee,
sweet oranges of Seville,
Californian wines and walnuts,
Moroccan
mint-tea.

Aisle, and aisle piled high
to stimulate, engage;
while artichokes, cabbage and sprouts,
place place-names
on our plates.

Coin-fed trolleys circle
corn-fed chicken wings
and hot bread warm aromas
entrap the passers-by
then, reddest red carnations,
with roses, sprigs and sprays
celebrate effusiveness
for all who care, but pay.

And toddler thinking
yummy mums
'side power dressed blond gazelles,
both Serengeti traversers
crave courtesy in queues.

For most, transient inconvenience;
for some, a therapy.

Holy Land

In God We Trust

We bartered chickens for turkeys
buffalo for horse, a handful of jangled trinkets
bought ten thousand acres and built how many
white houses for a twenty dollar bill?
What juggernaut of zeros built an Empire State
and was it real money, or just promised?

Germany in that second War
Printed barrow-loads just to buy bread
when paper value vanished-
gone where?
and all that printing, printing Yen, Renminbi,
Roubles, Pesos, Shekels.

Pipe-smoking, nasal-toned Harold Wilson
in his Gannex rain-coat told us about
the pound in our pocket, reassured us of its value.
The Bank of England Governor promised to pay the
bearer
One Pound Sterling, with the Royal visage imprinted
to attest reliability, trustworthiness, confidence.

Irish Ploughman notes, and Lady Lavery sometime
resting on her harp and my first pay-packet, of crisp
red
Twenty Pounders legally so tender, which I would
hide in a sock,
in a drawer, in a dingy bed-sit:
Later, Euros with ECB Governor signatures
replaced Escudos, Liras, Francs, Pesetas, even Punts.

In the City by-the-Bay where Mission meets Market
I saw them emerge at dusk, gaunt as walking dead.
They scavenged garbage baskets, retrieved plastic
bottles
to exchange for cash -
'I need a dollar', they mumble,
'a dollar is what I need', they say.

My gold was turned to alloy coin, decimalized,
turned to credit on a plastic card –
I buy in-store, on-line, by phone.
At every turn, I consume,
make all things right,
keep confidence,
believe.

Hells Angels

Thunderous roar
the machines belch fury
riders clad in black leathers
emblazoned crests, tattooed arms.

Make way for the high-kings of the road
make way, we come through.

Even the sidewalks tremble
on Main Street by Bath Place,
Blackrock, Dublin, Ireland.

Odyssey

Through dark inner-city streets
by ramshackle tenements,
dead-end courtyards, bricked-up doors,
deserted archaeological sites, a darkling,
I scurry to the coast to meet the dawn.

At the sea
a great river
cascades over
a precipice into
ocean's morning arms.

From the rocks a beachcomber waves,
invites me back to a beach-house den
where a motley crew distribute soft-flannel
jerseys, tightly fitted to pop at the neck,
with printed preachy logos, *'born-again'*.

I huddle in the corner of the clubhouse.
From my wallet I count out vouchers
for *Propter's Nicodemus Pills*,
Confederate notes, currency from *Zambesia*.
Guilty, I think, 'Should I give them all, would that be
enough'?

I fear I may be mugged,
by other kinds of people;
I overhear, 'He has a PhD'.

A raggle-taggle kinship in their shack

with corrugated tin-roof, wooden chairs,
bare trestle tables scattered round,
saying,
redemption.

Jericho

We were there 'round ninety two
when armed bus-guides warned
heat could kill,
so,
sun-screened, hippy-hatted, eye-shaded,
clutching bottled water in
searing sun and sweltering heat,
we stood in line
and gaped at excavated ruins
believing the wall went down below
as no wall stood above the ground
and we tried
to imagine a quake when
loud shouts, the blast of horns,
dislodged brick from rubble
and mud-brick from stone
so,
we stood in line and I thought of
Rahab's red cord, a line for
passing-over or
a line to connect
when records would show
a blood-line to a child
whose nature would destroy
veils, partitions, even walls.

High Hopes

I met old Abraham sitting on a bar stool in Tel Aviv
mumbling into his Americano coffee fumes about
unimaginable consequences as things converge.

Since Ur in Mesopotamia, where things started,
he had eight sons, but she laughed
at the special one, as she was old.

I asked were there genetic traits,
his children, their children, a nation numbered
as sea-shore sand-grains, and so on?

He inhaled the coffee aroma as the waiter topped-up
his mug.
I asked about the mountain, knife, the boy,
the altar, was there a voice or voices?

He mumbled again about irresistible convergence,
the ram, caught in the thicket, by its horns, if not for
the ram,
would history give us twelve tribes, twelve apostles?

Eventually, maybe six million people
would not be extinguished in the camps,
Unfathomable things, with consequences.

Mount of Olives

I bask in warm summer sun on this gentle hillside,
face upturned, eyes closed, see brightness through
closed lids
absorb warm kisses from the gentle air
my every fibre harmonized with the universe
as my spirit drinks wellness.

I try to detach sight, hearing, touch, smell and taste,
to imagine a reality beyond such limited senses
and with Elisha's prayer, see holy-hosts
encamped around to comfort and reassure
that God can breathe this air, being as one with it.

I flounder at reality detached from the corporeal and
in the end rest my hope only in a person
who walked dusty roads, shared bread and wine
with friends
on hillsides like this, but walked on water.

Jerusalem's Western Wall

Sheep, goats, hyenas scavenged here.
Now, no traffic sounds, no fumes choke; unclean
animals are restrained.

Pilgrim hands touch sand-grey and sand-brown
stones. Squinting eyes hide behind ray-bans,
foreheads and ears press stone, mouths kiss rock.

Black-robed Hasidic chanters hum, sway, pray for
peace within the walls, for prosperity, for plenty.

Skull-capped presidents place invocations, hopes,
requests in the cracks and crevices of our time.

Who knows their pleadings?
And all, on tiny scraps of paper, sufficient to hold a
world's prayers.

Notes on some of the Poems

My Fair City - the restored tenement house museum at 14 Henrietta Street Dublin provided some inspiration for this work along with the adjacent Kings Inns gardens. Established in 1541, King's Inns, Henrietta Street is Ireland's oldest school of law. Dublin's York Street tenements were demolished in the late 1960's being declared unfit for human habitation. The colour scheme for painting the corridors and hallways of Dublin tenements was frequently (Reckits) blue and (Raddle) red.

Christmas Eve, St Patrick's Cathedral, Dublin- the Latin phrases *'Expectans Espectavi Dominum'* trans; 'I waited for the Lord' in choral music by Irish composer Charles Wood (1866-1926) and C. Saint-Saëns (1835-1921) -'Oratorio de Noël'. *Hodie Christus Natus*; Trans; 'Today is Christ born' in early choral music by J.P. Sweelinck (1562-1621) and G. da Palestrina (c 1525-1594). 'Let them bring forth salvation' quote from Isaiah 45: 8.

Old James' Street Workhouse (1707-1826) – This 'House of Industry' offered housing for beggars, vagabonds, deserted children under the age of eight, and the mentally insane. It was also a foundling hospital taking in deserted infants in Dublin but owing to abnormally high mortality rates (four out of five) the foundling hospital came under scrutiny and investigation. These investigations found strong evidence of malpractice directly responsible for the death of thousands of children. The babies were deposited anonymously in a revolving cradle in the work house door. The British House of Commons stopped allowing new admissions to the hospital in 1831.

Brahms and Clara- Johannes Brahms (1833-1897) and Clara Schuman (1819-1896) wife of Robert Schuman were close and affectionate musical collaborators.

Glenstal Abbey-a Benedictine monastery in Murroe Co. Limerick which in addition to being a popular venue for retreats on occasions has hosted a series of organ Music Summer schools. Diapason and Dulciana are organ stops with soothing textures.

End of Day - the name given for marbles made from left over shards of glass.

The Lift- Since 1935 'Solus' light bulbs were manufactured by the Irish company of the same name at its one time located factory in Bray Co. Wicklow.

Baby Doherty- a victim of the Dublin bombing on 17 May 1974. In 2022 a further baby Martha O'Neill's name is to be added to the Talbot Street memorial; baby Martha was born still-born at full term 3 months after the bombing.

Just the way it was – references the assassination of President John Fitzgerald Kennedy 22nd November 1963 who had visited Ireland that same year to a rapturous welcome elevating him almost to sainthood amongst the general population. Walter Cronkite, concluded his final appearance as CBS Evening News anchor-man 6th March 1981 with his customary line 'And that's the way it is'. Charles Mitchell was RTE Chief Newscaster broadcasting between 1961-1984 when he retired.

Virus – instances writings about human resilience and survival in 'The Stand' by Stephen King; 'The Road' by Cormac McCarthy; 'The Grapes of Wrath' by John Steinbeck. Edward Michael "Bear" Grylls OBE is a British adventurer, writer, television presenter and survival expert.

Pathétique – Performance of Tchaikovsky's final Symphony No. 6 in B minor, Op. 74, at 'An Ceolaras Naisiunta' Dublin, Ireland, Monday 27 April, 1987. *Ritenuto* and *pppp,* are musical terms for slowing down and sounding very very softly.

Black Bobby - One of the fastest of small dog breeds, Jack Russell Terriers can run as fast as 48 km per hour, covering short distances in lightning bursts

Mackerel – Muriel MacDonagh (nee Gifford 1884-1917) drowned swimming off Shenick Island east of Skerries Co. Dublin. She was wife of Thomas MacDonagh of Cloughjordan Co. Tipperary, signatory to the Proclamation of the Irish Republic, executed 1916. Muriel was a sister of Grace Gifford who married J.M.Plunkett hours before his execution in 1916.

Gold Pelican - an emblem awarded to blood donors: The Irish Blood Transfusion Service provides regular donors with button-hole emblems to commemorate their achievements. After 20 donations a Pelican Gold pin is awarded. The pelican is seen as a self-sacrificing bird feeding her young with her own blood.

Deus Ex Machina- the Husqvarna Automower, a popular automated grass cutting machine regularly observed in the fields and gardens around Arklow Co. Wicklow.

Tango – Por Una Cabeza – music by Carlos Gardel in the movie Scent of a Woman (1992) starring Al Pacino who plays a blind character (Pacino winning an Academy Award for best actor in the role).

Percy – William Percy French (1854-1920) born at Cloonyquinn House, Co Roscommon. The Irish troubadour, entertainer, composer, poet, artist and one time student of Trinity College Dublin whose employments including being an 'inspector of drains' for the Irish board of works in Co. Cavan. Brendan O'Dowda (1925-2002), an Irish tenor, popularised the songs of Percy French. John Maunder and John Stainer, English Victorian composers of religious music popular with church choirs in the early 1900's.

Ukulele Bus Busk- Pope Frances visited Ireland in August 2018. His journey around Dublin city caused major traffic disruption and prevented cross city travel by some who had intended to participate in the Ukulele Bus Busk event organized in Dun Laoghaire, south of the city.

Dun Laoghaire Harbour- Captain John McNeill Boyd perished while attempting to rescue others in stricken vessels in the great storm of 1861. While a memorial monument is preserved on Dun Laoghaire Harbour East Pier, Boyd's remains, when eventually retrieved were buried in the grounds of St. Patrick's Cathedral Dublin; tradition tells that his devoted dog can sometime still be seen wandering in search of his lost master.

Mortality Tables – the Pacific Ocean can support the journey of an uninterrupted wave between the Antarctic and the Arctic circles.

Anna Akhmatova (1889-1966) - *In memoriam.* Born near Odessa is regarded as one of Russia's greatest Modernist poets she was persecuted and suppressed by the Stalinist state who executed and imprisoned members of her family in Leningrad and the Gulag.

Friendship- Dylan Thomas (1914-1953) Welsh Poet, writer of 'Do not go gentle into that good night'.

The Big Event - John Betjeman (1906-1984) in his 'Diary of a Church Mouse' takes a satirical review of church activities through the eyes of a mouse.

Ardens sed Virens – the moto of the Presbyterian Church in Ireland drawn from the story of the burning bush on Mount Horeb (Exodus Ch. 3). Burning but not extinguished. The giant Californian Redwood trees have proved resistant to forest fires.

Retail Therapy - Jerusalem artichokes, Savoy cabbage and Brussels sprouts.

In God we Trust - The motto 'In God We Trust' first appeared on the U.S. 2 cent piece in 1864 and has appeared on US Paper Currency since 1957. The US currency $20 bill features its seventh President, Andrew Jackson (1829–1837) who signed the Indian Removal Act 1830 which ultimately led to the Cherokee Trail of Tears.

Odyssey- *Propter's Nicodemus Pills* referenced by Edward Lear in 'Some Incidents in the Life of My Uncle Arly'. *Confederate* Notes after the US Civil War between the States (c.1861-1865) proved worthless. The country *Zambesia* no longer exists.

Jericho- Palestinian city in the West Bank said to be the city with the oldest known protective wall. The Israelites entering the land of Canaan captured the city some sources indicate c 1500 B.C. when the walls fell down. Rahab the prostitute was rescued in the sacking having hidden two Israelite spies. Rahab through marriage became an ancestor recorded in the genealogy of Christ (Matthew 1: 5).

High Hopes - the City of Ur in ancient Mesopotamia said to be the home of the Patriarch Abraham before he set out on his journey to the promised land of Canaan.

Mount of Olives – Mountain ridge near Jerusalem said to be the place where Jesus ascended to heaven (Acts 1: 9-12). Site of the 'Mount of Olives Jewish Cemetery'.

Jerusalem's Western Wall - Hasidic - a pietistic group within Judaism.

About the Author

Derek Seymour studied poetry and attended workshops/
masterclasses with Lucinda Jacob, Leo Cullen, and Robert
Pinsky and was a founding member of the Carraig Dubh
Writers Group in Blackrock Co. Dublin. A first prize
winner of the 2018 ICWF Poetry Competition, he was
selected for the Stinging Fly 2018 Poetry Summer School -
leader Martina Evans with Siobhan Campbell. He
achieved second place in 'Dalkey Creates' 2020
International Poetry Competition. In addition to writing,
following his retirement from the Banking industry he is
involved with a number of voluntary sector charities. He
holds music qualifications in both Organ and Piano and
for many years has been organist and director of music at
Methodist Centenary Church Dublin. He lives in Dun
Laoghaire, Co. Dublin, Ireland and is married to the
playwright and actor Rose Henderson; they have four
children.

Index of Titles

Index of First Lines

Printed in Great Britain
by Amazon